PARTS OF SPEECH
COLORING COMIC WORKBOOK

This book is the future masterpiece of:

_____

Copyright © 2022 Amanda Hargen

All rights reserved. No part of this book may be reproduced or used in any manner without the prior written permission of the copyright owner, except for the use of brief quotations in a book review.

To request permissions, contact the publisher at maskedmotif@super-ela.com.

Readers should be aware that web addresses offered as sources for further information may have changed or disappeared between when this was written and when it is read.

ISBN 979-8-218-03745-1

First paperback edition August 2022.

SUPER ELA!
www.super-ela.com

For Steve

About SUPER ELA!

SUPER ELA! is the passion project of Amanda Hargen, a goofy English teacher-turned-cartoonist. It was born out of her desire to improve her students' grammar in a way that didn't bore them to tears. If you have any inquiries pertaining to **SUPER ELA!**, please send them to **maskedmotif@super-ela.com**.

TABLE OF CONTENTS

How to Use This Book vi
Why Learn the Parts of Speech? 1
Nouns 3
      Common Nouns 4
      Proper Nouns 5
Pronouns 6
      Personal Pronouns (Subject and Object) 7
      Than vs. As Rule 8
      Possessive Pronouns 9
Verbs 10
      Verb Tenses 11
      Linking Verbs 12
Adjectives 15
Adverbs 18
Conjunctions 21
Prepositions 24
      Prepositional Phrases 25
Interjections 27
Answer Key 30
Super Secret Bonus Content 36

HOW TO USE THIS BOOK

This isn't just a book about grammar. It's so much more than that! It's also a **coloring book**. These pages are yours to color and mark up as you see fit.

WHAT IS A NOUN?

A FEW NOTES ABOUT THE FORMAT:

- **Bolded** words are important terms.
- Boxes in ALL CAPS contain definitions and explanations.
- Boxes in lowercase are examples.
- The 🧠 symbol means that there's a **brain challenge**. Brain challenges provide opportunities for you to review and extend what you've learned.

Don't let the parts of speech be dull and lifeless. Add a little color!

Need some coloring inspiration? Head over to the **Terms** section of www.super-ela.com to check out colored versions of these comics!

GET YOUR COLORS READY...

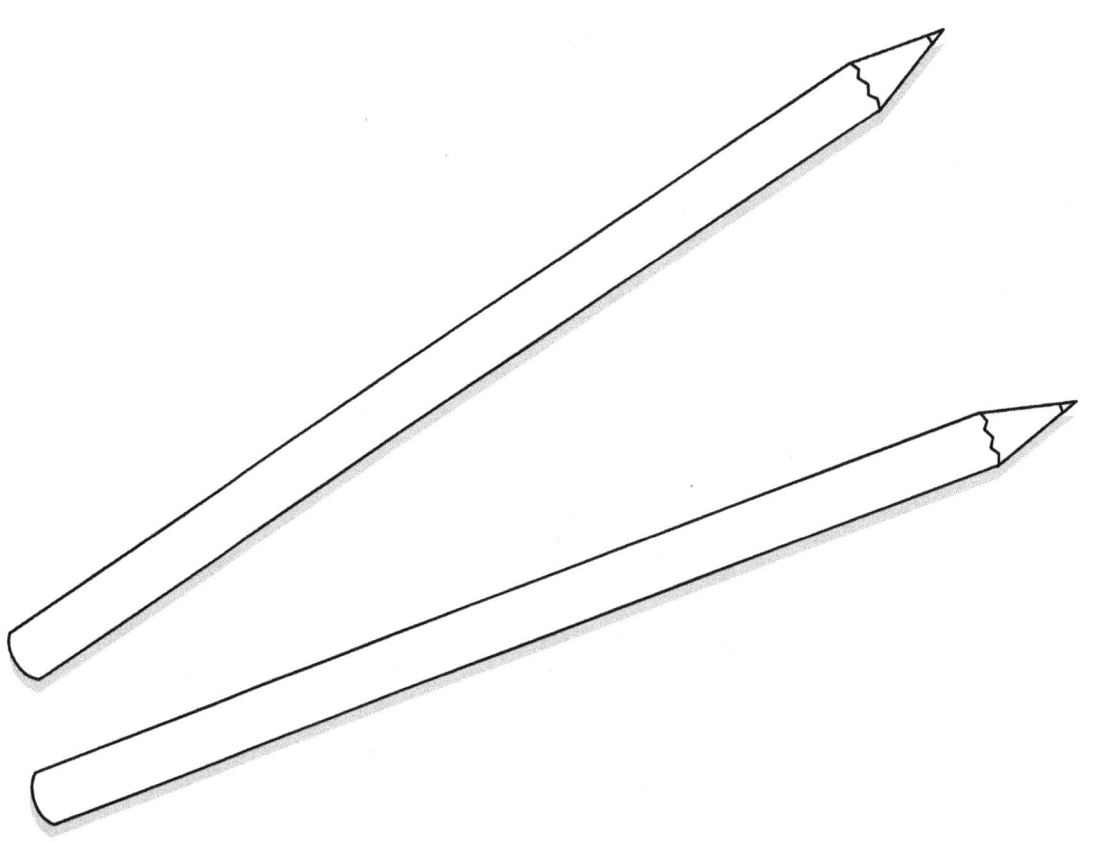

FIRST THINGS FIRST... WHY THE PARTS OF SPEECH?

IS LEARNING THE **PARTS OF SPEECH** A WASTE OF TIME? NO! KNOWING YOUR **NOUNS, PRONOUNS, VERBS, ADJECTIVES, ADVERBS, CONJUNCTIONS, PREPOSITIONS,** AND **INTERJECTIONS** CAN HELP YOU CRAFT STRONG SENTENCES THAT STAND THE TEST OF TIME.

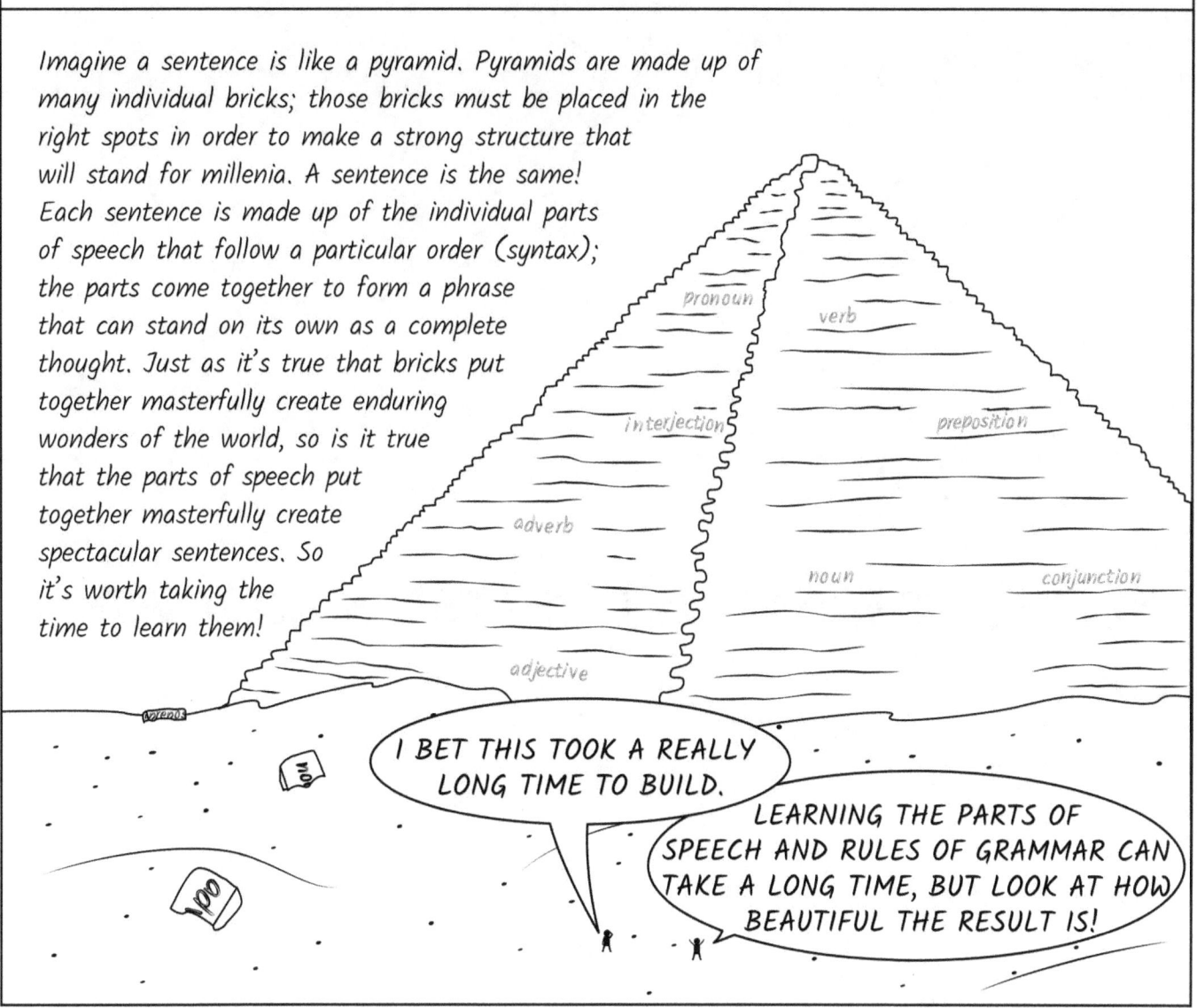

Imagine a sentence is like a pyramid. Pyramids are made up of many individual bricks; those bricks must be placed in the right spots in order to make a strong structure that will stand for millenia. A sentence is the same! Each sentence is made up of the individual parts of speech that follow a particular order (syntax); the parts come together to form a phrase that can stand on its own as a complete thought. Just as it's true that bricks put together masterfully create enduring wonders of the world, so is it true that the parts of speech put together masterfully create spectacular sentences. So it's worth taking the time to learn them!

Take a moment to create an inventory, or list, of what you already know about the parts of speech:

I know that _____

_____

Is there anything you wish you knew about the parts of speech? List what you'd like to learn here:

_____

_____

NOW LET'S DIG INTO THE PARTS OF SPEECH, STARTING WITH...

WHAT IS A NOUN?

EXERCISE 1 — Directions: Circle the **32 nouns** in the passage below. Check your answers on page 30.

There was once a rhinoceros named Dave. He was a sweet pachyderm, unlike his brothers, Luke and William. While his siblings roamed the savanna looking for trouble in the form of taunting zebras and harassing lions, Dave spent his time planting a lovely garden and chatting with his neighbors, the wildebeest and the ostrich. He was especially nice to the warthog, as he admired her beautiful tusks and stately gait. To show his admiration, Dave brought the warthog bouquets of flowers and sweet grasses. Because of these actions, Dave earned the reputation of being the nicest beast in the region.

WHAT IS A COMMON NOUN?

EXERCISE 2   **Directions:** Add one or more **common nouns** to each category. Read suggested answers on page 30.

1. flamingo, ostrich, owl, hummingbird, _____

2. carrot, lettuce, potato, pepper, _____

3. cow, pig, horse, sheep, _____

4. cheddar, provolone, mozzarella, parmesan, _____

5. fish, narwhal, whale, seahorse, _____

WHAT IS A PROPER NOUN?

PERSON — Jack Hanna

Fun Fact: Famous zookeeper Jack Hanna once got stuck in an airport turnstile with a flamingo. Yikes!

PLACE — The Everglades

A **PROPER NOUN** IS THE NAME OF A PARTICULAR PERSON, PLACE, THING, OR IDEA. PROPER NOUNS ARE CAPITALIZED.

THING — Flamingo (statue)

The "Flamingo" sculpture in Chicago, designed by Alexander Calder, towers 53 feet over the sidewalk. It's painted bright red!

IDEA — Kemetism (hieroglyph for "sun")

Kemetism is the modern belief in ancient Egyptian gods. Did you know that the Egyptians of old viewed flamingos as a symbol of Ra, their god of the sun?

See a picture of the real statue at https://www.super-ela.com/flamingo-statue/.

EXERCISE 3

Directions: Match each **proper noun** on the left with a corresponding **common noun** on the right. Check your answers on page 30.

1. Green Bay Packers
2. Australia
3. Ludwig van Beethoven
4. Mississippi River
5. Loch Ness Monster

a. composer
b. country
c. mythical creature
d. team
e. river

Brain Challenge: How would you explain **nouns** to a friend? Without referencing the nouns comics, write your answer below. Check your knowledge when you're finished.

_____

_____

_____

www.super-ela.com/terms/nouns

WHAT IS A PRONOUN?

A **PRONOUN** TAKES THE PLACE OF A NOUN. THE WORD OR GROUP OF WORDS TO WHICH THE PRONOUN REFERS IS THE **ANTECEDENT**.

A chimpanzee named David Greybeard changed the world's view of primate intelligence when **he** was observed using tall grasses to extract termites from a hill.

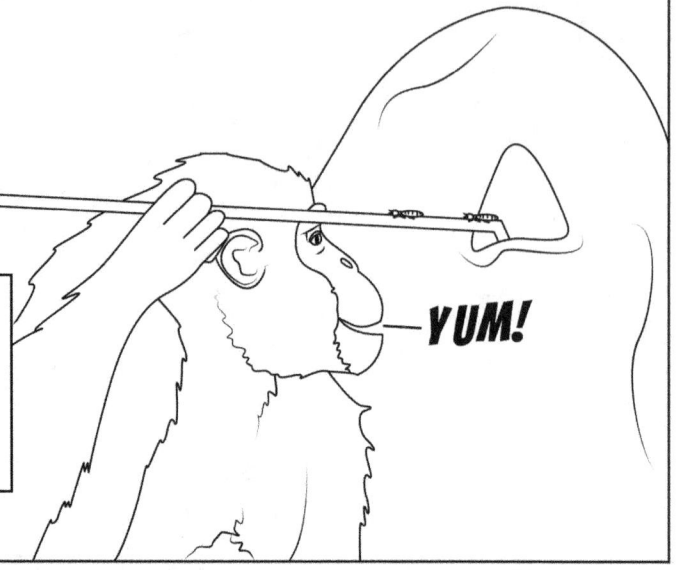
—YUM!

WHY DO WE USE PRONOUNS?
THEY PREVENT SENTENCES FROM SOUNDING REPETITIVE.

IN THE SENTENCE ABOVE, THE PRONOUN **HE** REPLACES THE ANTECEDENT **DAVID GREYBEARD** SO IT ISN'T USED TWICE.

A **PERSONAL PRONOUN** REFERS TO A SPECIFIC PERSON OR THING. IT INDICATES THE SPEAKER (**1ST PERSON**), THE PERSON BEING ADDRESSED (**2ND PERSON**), OR ANOTHER PERSON OR THING BEING DISCUSSED (**3RD PERSON**).

1ST PERSON

I hope that chimp doesn't want to kiss **me**.

2ND PERSON

You can't imagine how strong chimps are.

3RD PERSON

Jane Goodall studied chimps; **she** found **them** fascinating.

Brain Challenge: Read and color the comic above. Then cover it with a piece of paper. Next, write down everything you can remember about **pronouns** on the lines below. No peeking! Check your knowledge when you're finished.

_____
_____
_____
_____

www.super-ela.com/terms/pronouns

PERSONAL PRONOUNS EXPRESS **NUMBER**, AS THEY CAN BE **SINGULAR** (ONE) OR **PLURAL** (MANY).

3RD PERSON PERSONAL PRONOUNS CAN ALSO EXPRESS GENDER. **HE** AND **HIM** ARE MASCULINE, **SHE** AND **HER** ARE FEMININE, AND **IT** IS NEUTER (NEITHER).

PERSONAL PRONOUNS	SINGULAR	PLURAL
1ST PERSON	I, me	we, us
2ND PERSON	you	you
3RD PERSON	he, him, she, her, it, they*	they, them

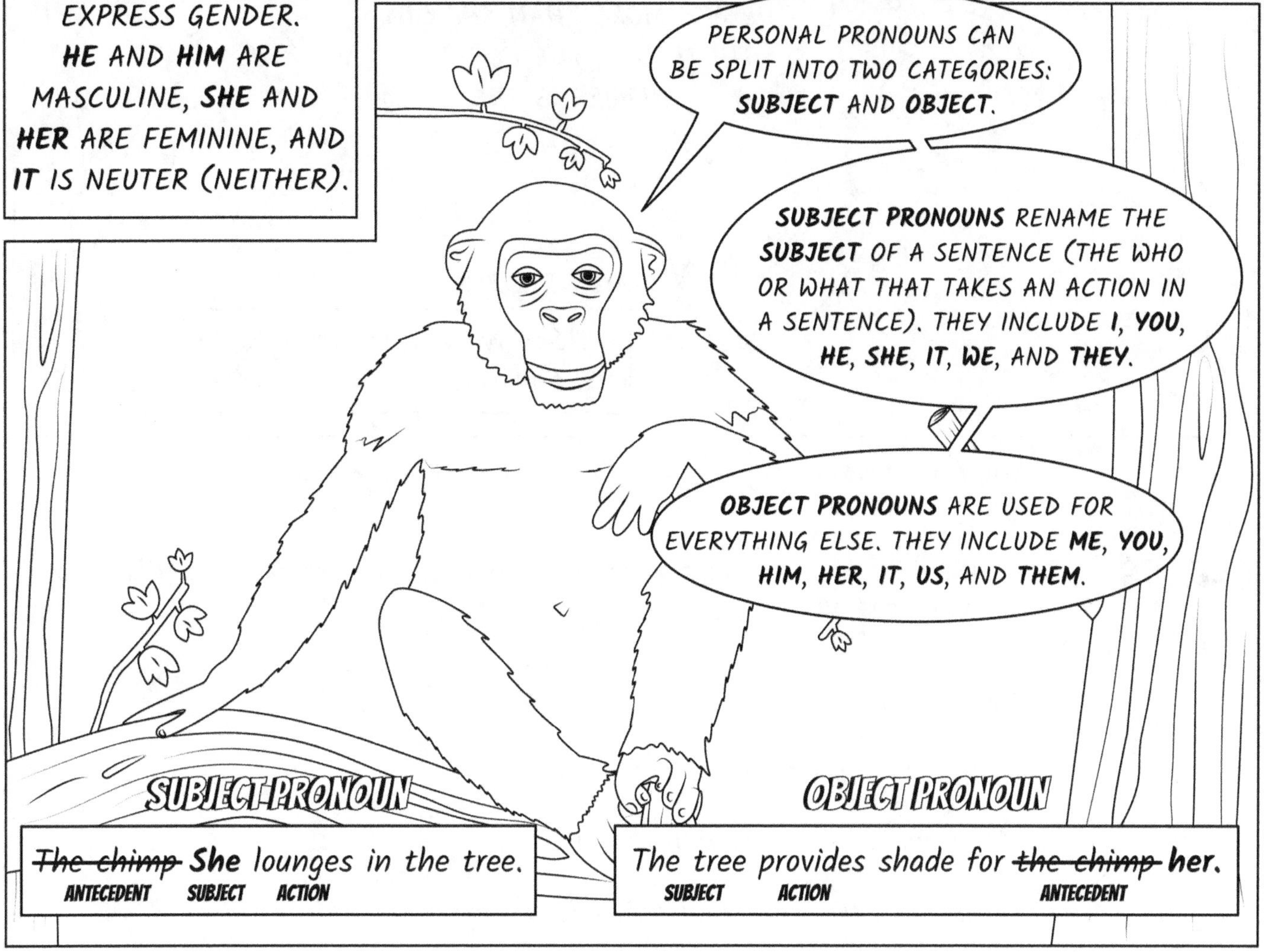

PERSONAL PRONOUNS CAN BE SPLIT INTO TWO CATEGORIES: **SUBJECT** AND **OBJECT**.

SUBJECT PRONOUNS RENAME THE **SUBJECT** OF A SENTENCE (THE WHO OR WHAT THAT TAKES AN ACTION IN A SENTENCE). THEY INCLUDE **I**, **YOU**, **HE**, **SHE**, **IT**, **WE**, AND **THEY**.

OBJECT PRONOUNS ARE USED FOR EVERYTHING ELSE. THEY INCLUDE **ME**, **YOU**, **HIM**, **HER**, **IT**, **US**, AND **THEM**.

SUBJECT PRONOUN
~~The chimp~~ **She** lounges in the tree.
ANTECEDENT   SUBJECT   ACTION

OBJECT PRONOUN
The tree provides shade for ~~the chimp~~ **her**.
SUBJECT   ACTION   ANTECEDENT

Brain Challenge: Write one sentence that uses a **subject pronoun**, and write another sentence that uses an **object pronoun**. Use the examples above as models for your sentences.

_____

_____

_____

Possible answers:
1) **They** love playing in the park. (Subject Pronoun - **They** takes the place of the specific names of people in the group.)
2) The chimpanzee waved to **him**. (Object Pronoun - **Him** takes the place of a specific person's name.)

* Read an explanation of the **singular they** at www.super-ela.com/terms/pronouns

IT CAN BE TRICKY TO CHOOSE THE CORRECT PRONOUN WHEN IT FOLLOWS **THAN** OR **AS**. YOU CAN FIGURE OUT WHICH TO CHOOSE BY MENTALLY COMPLETING THE SENTENCE.

FOR EXAMPLE
He ate more than **she**.

IF YOU MENTALLY COMPLETE THE SENTENCE, IT WOULD BE "HE ATE MORE THAN **SHE DID**." THEREFORE, THE CORRECT ANSWER IS **SHE**.

ANOTHER EXAMPLE
She wasn't as hungry as **he**.
(She wasn't as hungry as **he was**.)

(We don't tend to observe this rule in spoken English, but it is grammatically correct.)

EXERCISE 4 **Directions:** Choose the correct **personal pronoun(s)** for each sentence. Check your answers on page 30.

1. **She / her** loves karate.

2. **They / them** prefer goat cheese pizza.

3. Gloria and John walked with **they / them**.

4. **I / me** hope that tiger isn't following **we / us**.

5. Eloise taunted **he / him**, but **we / us** put a stop to it.

6. Can you ask **she / her** if **she / her** will go to the movies with **I / me**?

7. **He / him** is less agile than **she / her**.

8. Have you seen my bicycle? I can't find **it / him**.

www.super-ela.com/terms/pronouns

A POSSESSIVE PRONOUN TAKES THE PLACE OF A POSSESSIVE FORM OF A NOUN. IT INDICATES OWNERSHIP OR POSSESSION. SOME POSSESSIVE PRONOUNS ARE USED BEFORE NOUNS, WHILE OTHERS CAN BE USED BY THEMSELVES.

POSSESSIVE PRONOUNS	SINGULAR	PLURAL
1ST PERSON	my, mine	our, ours
2ND PERSON	your, yours	your, yours
3RD PERSON	his, her, hers, their, its	their, theirs

POSSESSIVE NOUN
The **chimp's** selfishness was unparalleled.

POSSESSIVE PRONOUN
His selfishness was unparalleled.

"This tree is **mine**!"

Chimps are known for **their** selfish behavior.

EXERCISE 5

Directions: Fix any **pronoun** errors in the following sentences. Some corrections require **personal pronouns**, while others require **possessive pronouns**. Place a check (✓) next to sentences that are correct. Check your answers on page 31.

1. Us must return this lost jacket to it's owner.

2. This cardigan is mine!

3. There potato salad is the best me have ever tasted!

4. He's basketball jersey is in the washing machine.

5. You're mom told me mom to tell I to tell your that her is making a casserole for dinner.

www.super-ela.com/terms/pronouns

WHAT IS A VERB?

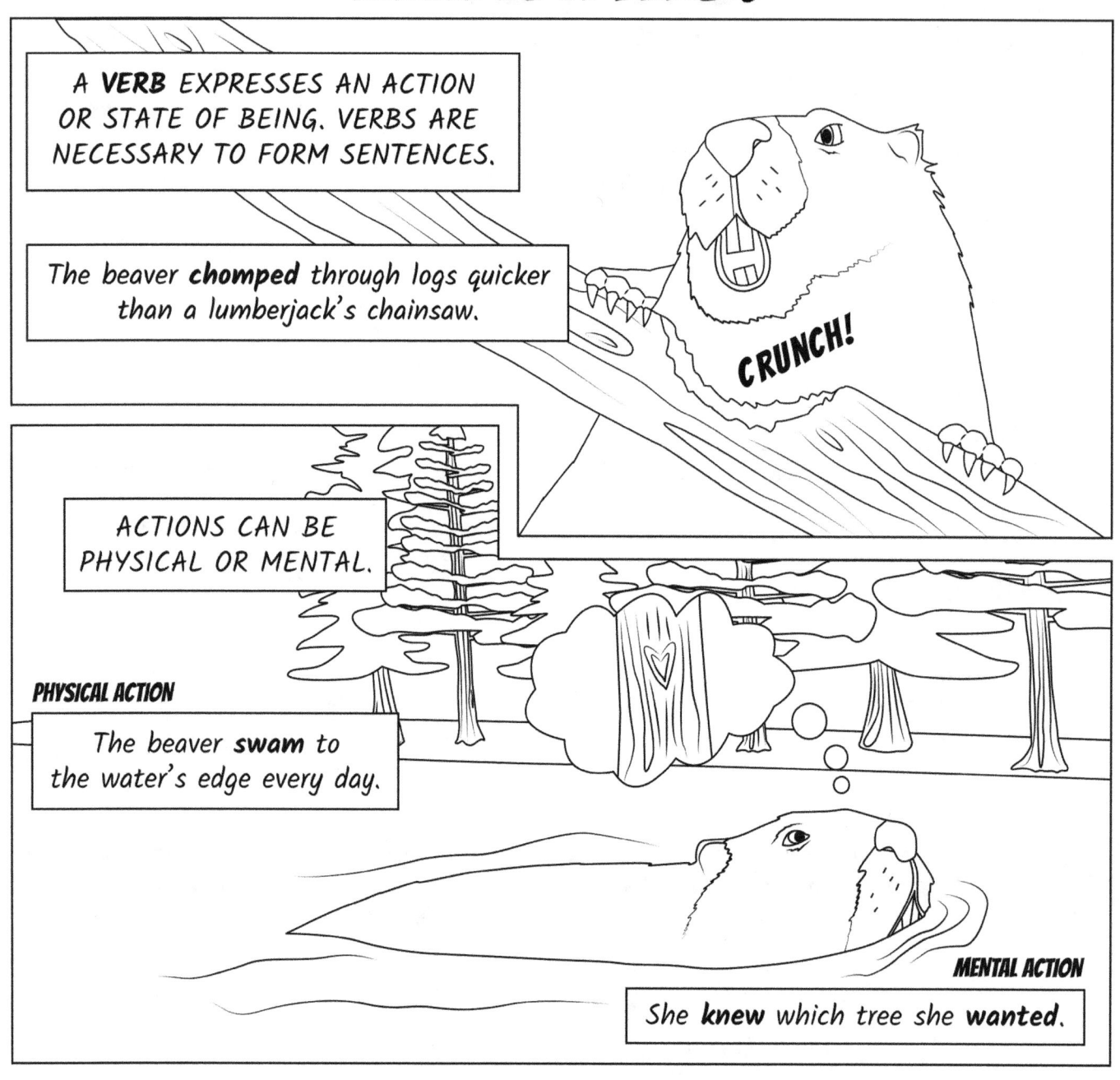

A **VERB** EXPRESSES AN ACTION OR STATE OF BEING. VERBS ARE NECESSARY TO FORM SENTENCES.

The beaver **chomped** through logs quicker than a lumberjack's chainsaw.

CRUNCH!

ACTIONS CAN BE PHYSICAL OR MENTAL.

PHYSICAL ACTION
The beaver **swam** to the water's edge every day.

MENTAL ACTION
She **knew** which tree she **wanted**.

Brain Challenge: Write down as many words for **mental** and **physical actions** as you can. Try to fill the lines below!

_____
_____
_____
_____

Possible answers: run, walk, jump, skip, hop, read, think, leap, dance, roll, clap, stomp, talk, cry

Past tense verbs describe actions that already happened, present tense verbs describe actions that are happening right now, and future tense verbs describe actions that haven't happened yet.

EXERCISE 6   **Directions:** Circle the **verbs** that appear in the following sentences. Then identify if they are written in the **past tense**, **present tense**, or **future tense**. Check your answers on page 31.

1. Denise bakes bread every morning at five o'clock.
2. She perfected her recipe over many years of practice.
3. Denise sells her bread in a little shop on the edge of town.
4. In the morning, her store will bustle with customers.
5. The townspeople love her bread; it tastes of cinnamon!
6. Only one person—a stranger—expressed dislike for the cinnamon bread.
7. He had a cinnamon allergy.
8. Denise will think about how to help this stranger.
9. She created a cinnamon-free loaf.
10. The stranger thanked her, paid for the bread, and scarfed it down.

www.super-ela.com/terms/verbs

A **LINKING VERB** IS A VERB THAT DOES NOT EXPRESS AN ACTION. INSTEAD, IT **LINKS** THE SUBJECT OF THE SENTENCE TO A WORD OR PHRASE THAT IDENTIFIES OR DESCRIBES IT. **TO BE** IS THE MOST COMMON LINKING VERB.

FORMS OF TO BE

PRESENT TENSE:	PAST TENSE:	PAST PARTICIPLE:	PRESENT PARTICIPLE:
AM, IS, ARE	WAS, WERE	HAVE BEEN	BEING

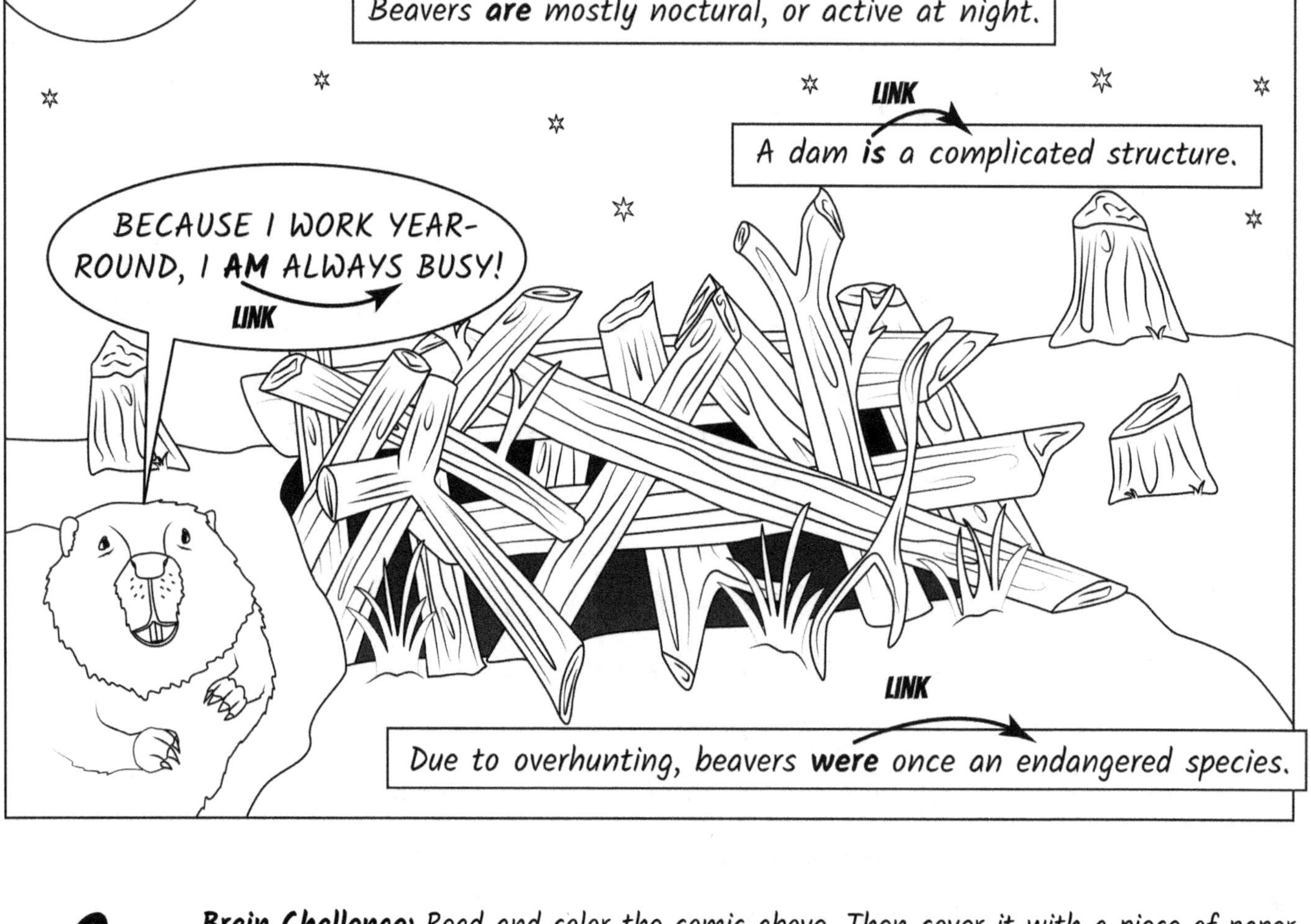

Beavers **are** mostly noctural, or active at night. *(LINK)*

A dam **is** a complicated structure. *(LINK)*

BECAUSE I WORK YEAR-ROUND, I **AM** ALWAYS BUSY! *(LINK)*

Due to overhunting, beavers **were** once an endangered species. *(LINK)*

Brain Challenge: Read and color the comic above. Then cover it with a piece of paper. Next, think about how you would explain **linking verbs** to a friend. Write your answer on the lines below. No peeking! Check your knowledge when you're finished.

_____
_____
_____

COMMON LINKING VERBS

appear	look	seem	stay
become	grow	smell	taste
feel	remain	sound	

HOW TO TELL IF IT'S LINKING OR ACTION

ASK YOURSELF THE FOLLOWING QUESTION:

WILL THE SENTENCE STILL MAKE SENSE IF I REPLACE THE **VERB** WITH **AM**, **IS**, OR **ARE**?

IF THE ANSWER IS YES

IT'S A **LINKING VERB**!

The beavers **feel** sleepy after a feast of twigs and branches.

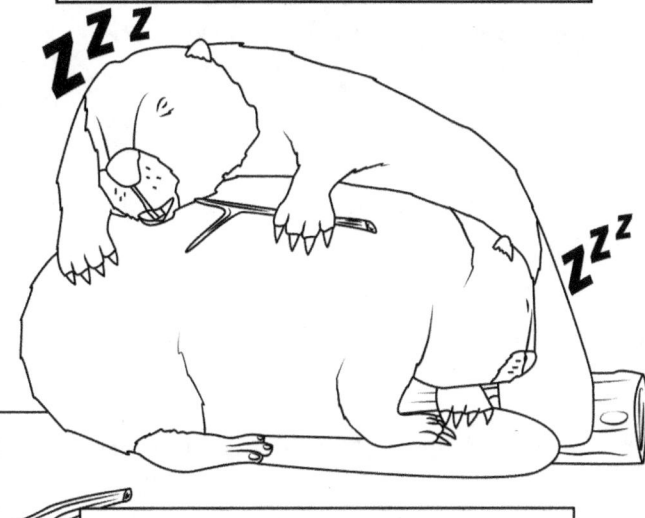

THE BEAVERS **ARE** SLEEPY? YES, THAT MAKES SENSE! THIS IS A LINKING VERB.

IF THE ANSWER IS NO

IT'S AN **ACTION VERB**!

The eldest beaver **felt** a splinter in his paw.

THE ELDEST BEAVER **IS** A SPLINTER? NOPE! THIS IS AN ACTION VERB.

Brain Challenge: Write two sentences using **common linking verbs**. Try to use one as a **linking verb** and one as an **action verb**.

_____

_____

_____

Possible answers:
1) "I **feel** sick today." This works as a linking verb because you can replace **feel** with **am**.
2) "The cat **looks** at the dog with indifference." This works as an action verb because the cat is taking the action of looking.

www.super-ela.com/terms/verbs

EXERCISE 7 **Directions:** Use a form of **to be** to complete each of the following sentences. Check your answers on page 31.

1. On average, Florida _____ one of the hottest states in the U.S.

2. Zora Neale Hurston, a noted writer of the Harlem Renaissance, _____ an award-winning author who wrote classics like <u>Their Eyes Were Watching God</u>.

3. Killer whales, also called orcas, _____ misunderstood for many years, likely owing to their menacing name.

4. This is hard to admit, but I _____ afraid of Jell-O and other gelatinous desserts.

5. Bees _____ important for the world's ecosystem, as they help pollinate crops.

6. Despite the fact that it _____ enormous—weighing in at over 30,000lbs—the Tyrannosaurus rex's arms were only three feet long.

7. Socrates, Plato, and Aristotle _____ Greek philosophers who lived more than 2,400 years ago.

EXERCISE 8 **Directions:** Circle the **verbs** in each of the sentences below. Identify each as **action** or **linking**. Check your answers on page 32. The first one has been done for you.

1. Much to her surprise, Regina (thought) the seaweed and clam chowder (tasted) delicious.
                                        ACTION   LINKING

2. Torrey feels bored after three hours of notetaking in Mr. Bertram's history class.

3. An enormous talking robot appeared to Regan in a dream; he claimed his name was "Optimus Prime," but his nametag read "Larry."

4. To Elijah the field of daisies seemed endless; in reality, it was a small garden in his backyard.

5. Heather tasted a small bite of the raw fish before deciding that it was safe to eat.

6. Seconds from sleep, Eloise felt her mother place the soft blanket over her.

7. With contents like moldy socks and putrefied cabbage, it was no wonder that the garbage in the alleyway smelled rotten.

WHAT IS AN ADJECTIVE?

AN **ADJECTIVE** IS A WORD THAT DESCRIBES A NOUN OR PRONOUN; IT TELLS **WHAT KIND, WHICH ONE, HOW MANY,** OR **HOW MUCH.**

WHICH ONE → The **drowsy** koala soaked
HOW MANY → in a **single** ray of sunshine
WHAT KIND → during an **afternoon** nap.

ADJECTIVES CAN BE **POSITIVE, COMPARATIVE,** OR **SUPERLATIVE.**

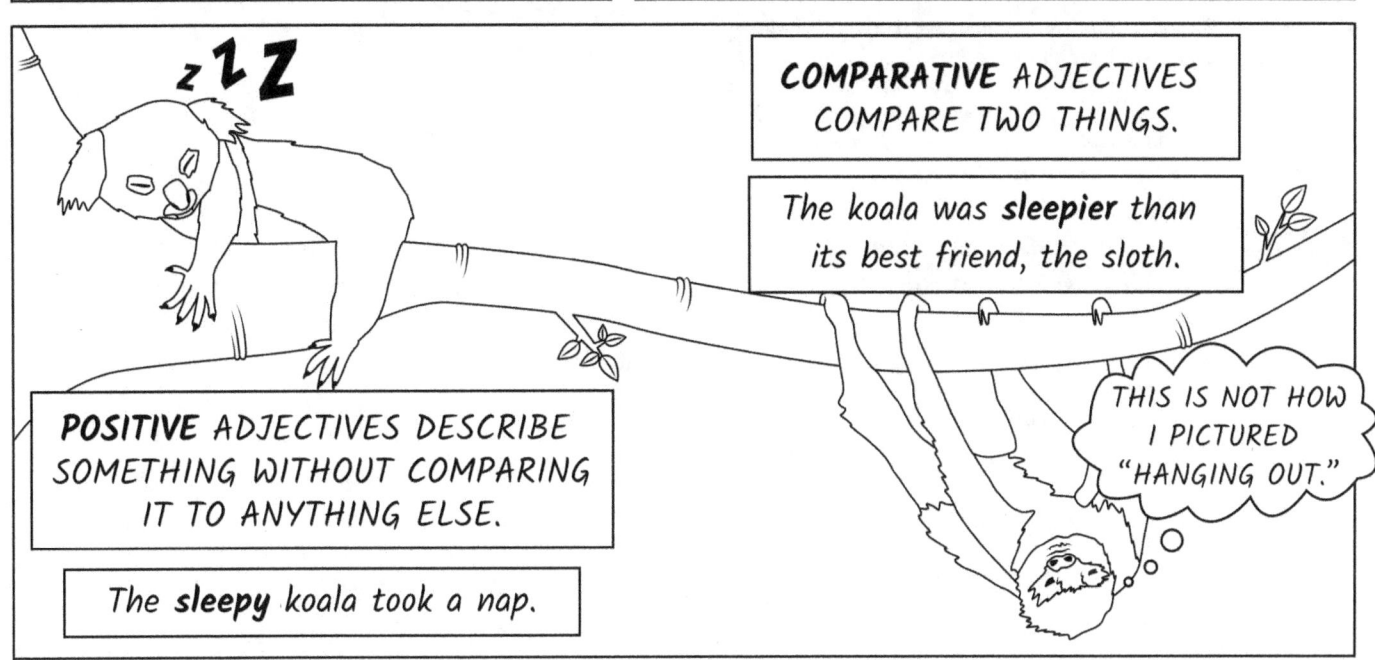

COMPARATIVE ADJECTIVES COMPARE TWO THINGS.

The koala was **sleepier** than its best friend, the sloth.

POSITIVE ADJECTIVES DESCRIBE SOMETHING WITHOUT COMPARING IT TO ANYTHING ELSE.

The **sleepy** koala took a nap.

THIS IS NOT HOW I PICTURED "HANGING OUT."

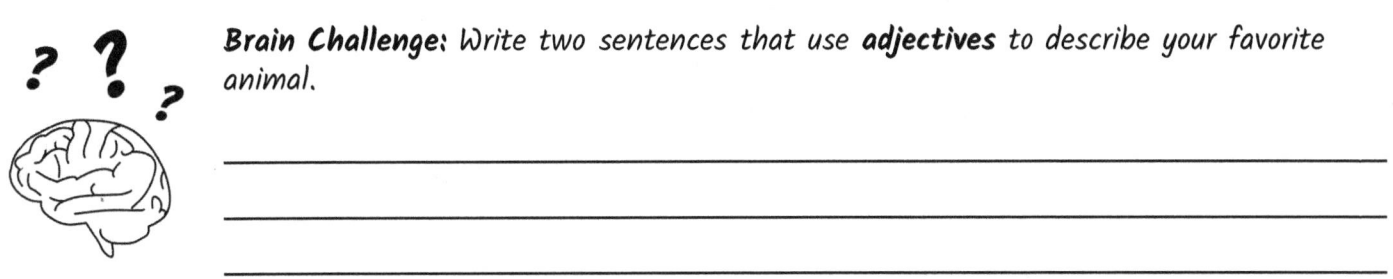

Brain Challenge: Write two sentences that use **adjectives** to describe your favorite animal.

_____
_____
_____

Possible answers: 1) My poodle is **black** and **fuzzy**. 2) He is **lazy** and loves sleeping on **soft** pillows.

www.super-ela.com/terms/adjectives

Note: While many adjectives follow the structure of **sleepy**, **sleepier**, and **sleepiest**, some are irregular. For example, the comparative form of **good** is **better**, and the superlative form is **best**. Some adjectives add **more** or **most** to create the comparative and superlative forms. Use a dictionary to help you figure out the forms of a particular adjective!

EXERCISE 9   Directions: Circle the **adjectives** in the following sentences. (Note that **nouns** and **possessive pronouns** can act as adjectives!) Check your answers on page 32.

1. A sweet smell wafted through the air.
2. Was it chocolate cookies or fresh brownies?
3. Caroline couldn't tell, but she knew she wanted whatever delicious treat was in the kitchen.
4. She crept, silent as a mouse, toward the open kitchen door.
5. Her mom stooped in front of their enormous oven, pulling out a mystery pan from its warm interior.
6. Mom didn't know little Caroline was hiding by the door.
7. When she turned around and saw creepy eyes peering from the black hallway, she was startled.
8. She dropped the entire tray of cookies on the kitchen floor.
9. "Oh no!" Caroline cried as she emerged to help her mother pick up the broken cookies.
10. "Thank you, Caroline," her mom said with a disappointed note in her voice.

EXERCISE 10 **Directions:** Complete the sentences in each group by writing the correct **positive**, **comparative**, and **superlative** forms of the given adjective. Check your answers on page 32.

Tasty

1. Yesterday's lunch was _____.
2. It was the _____ of all the lunches I've ever eaten!
3. Is your lunch _____ than mine?

Great

4. Four is _____ than five.
5. Of all the numbers between one and infinity, which is the _____?
6. Thirteen is not a _____ number when it comes to luck!

Strong

7. Hercules was the _____ of the Greek heroes.
8. He was _____ than Achilles because he didn't have a weak ankle.
9. Though he was _____, he wasn't very bright.

Good

10. Gerald wanted to be _____ at math than his brother, Hank.
11. Unfortunately for Gerald, Hank was the _____ mathlete in the nation, so he was going to be hard to beat.
12. Gerald settled for just being _____ at math.

Inventive

13. Natalie was an _____ child.
14. She wanted to push her abilities so that she would be _____ than her hero, Nikola Tesla.
15. "Someday," she thought, "I'll be the _____ scientist the world has ever seen!

WHAT IS AN ADVERB?

AN **ADVERB** DESCRIBES A VERB, AN ADJECTIVE, OR ANOTHER ADVERB; IT MAKES THE MEANING MORE SPECIFIC BY EXPLAINING **HOW**, **WHEN**, **WHERE**, **WHY**, **HOW OFTEN**, AND **HOW MUCH**.

HEY! OVER HERE! HI, CAMPER!

MODIFYING A VERB

HOW OFTEN →
The bear **always** waved **gleefully** at campers.
VERB ← HOW

UH OH

MODIFYING AN ADJECTIVE

HOW MUCH → HOW MUCH →
The bear was **very** friendly and **basically** harmless.
ADJECTIVE — ADJECTIVE

Brain Challenge: Read and color the comic above. When you are finished, cover it with a piece of paper. Next, think about how you would explain **adverbs** to a friend. Write your answer on the lines below. No peeking! Check your knowledge when you're finished.

_____
_____
_____

www.super-ela.com/terms/adverbs

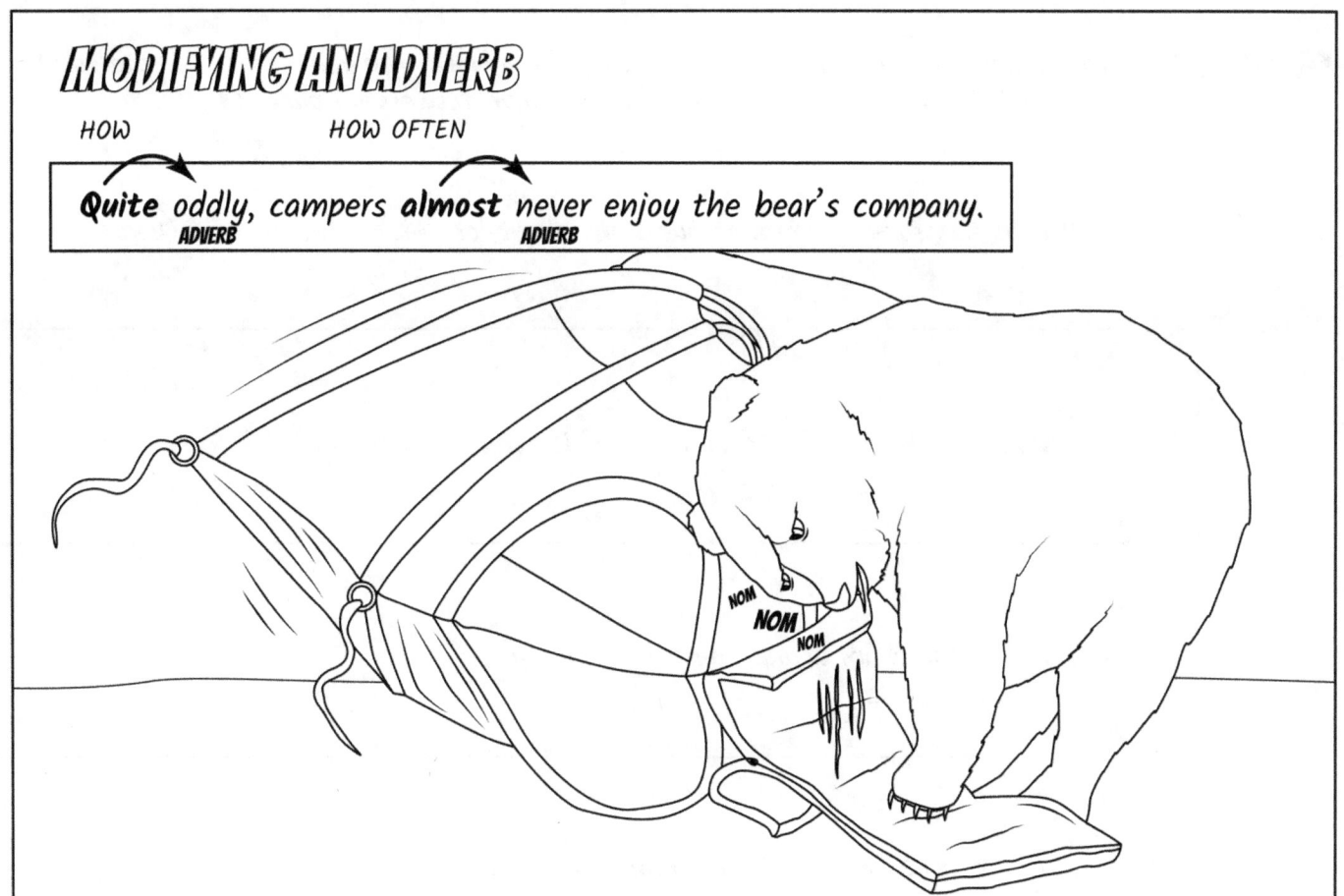

MODIFYING AN ADVERB

EXERCISE 11   **Directions:** Circle the word that is being modified or described by the **bolded adverb** in each sentence. Next, identify the part of speech of the circled word. The first one has been done for you. Check your answers on page 33.

1. The bear (smiled) **politely** at the camper, hoping it would ease her fear.
   VERB

2. You are **almost** always welcome to eat at our house; the only exception is when we have company.

3. The platypus is an **extremely** curious creature with its avian nose and mammalian body.

4. In addition to synchronized swimming, Janine **also** enjoys spelunking, or cave diving.

5. Ariel is **often** considered the most talented ballerina in her class.

www.super-ela.com/terms/adverbs

EXERCISE 12 Directions: Rewrite each sentence, adding the **adverb** in parentheses. Be sure to place the adverb in an appropriate position. Check your answers on page 33.

1. Marcus has some interesting questions about last night's homework. (very)

   _____

2. I wonder if there is a perfect flavor of ice cream. (sometimes)

   _____

3. The alligator swam across the pond. (slowly)

   _____

4. It is wise to save money for a rainy day. (generally)

   _____

5. The pizza was hot, and the cheese burned the roof of Andrew's mouth. (extremely)

   _____

6. I never eat breakfast in bed. (almost)

   _____

WHAT IS A CONJUNCTION?

CONJUNCTIONS ARE WORDS THAT JOIN SINGLE WORDS OR GROUPS OF WORDS. THE MOST BASIC KIND OF CONJUNCTION IS CALLED A **COORDINATING CONJUNCTION**.

AN EASY ACRONYM FOR REMEMBERING YOUR COORDINATING CONJUNCTIONS IS **FANBOYS**.

F	A	N	B	O	Y	S
for	and	nor	but	or	yet	so

The owl wanted to take off, **but** its feathers were too wet.

It was cold **and** snowy outside, **yet** Wilhemina could only think warm thoughts.

Owl always love you.

Brain Challenge: Write two sentences using **coordinating conjunctions** to describe your favorite and least favorite foods. Try to use three of the **FANBOYS**.

_____

_____

_____

Possible answers: 1) I love pizza, **but** I dislike pepperoni. 2) I can't eat broccoli, **so** I eat cauliflower **and** spinach instead.

www.super-ela.com/terms/conjunctions

EXERCISE 13 Directions: Circle the **coordinating conjunctions** in the sentences below. Check your answers on page 33.

1. Sookie wore a beautiful hat trimmed with white and green feathers.
2. The cat wanted to eat the mouse, yet she was too lazy to get up.
3. Dante was fluent in Spanish but not in French.
4. Regina couldn't decide if she wanted three cookies or four cookies, so she just ate seven cookies.
5. The elephant cried all morning, for it had a chipped tusk.
6. Bernard couldn't sing, nor could he dance.

EXERCISE 14 **Directions:** Add an appropriate **coordinating conjunction** to each of the blanks below. Check your answers on page 34.

1. Chloe wasn't cold, _____ was she hot.

2. Lightning split the old oak tree in two, _____ it had to be removed.

3. I want to do my homework, _____ I can't because I'm watching television!

4. Flamingos are usually a combination of white _____ pink; they become pinker if they eat more shrimp!

5. The dogs looked pleadingly at their owner, _____ it was time for dinner.

6. Daniel couldn't decide if he wanted to dye his hair navy _____ aqua.

7. The ground was frozen _____ hard, _____ it was not a good time to install a fence.

8. Tracy tried to eat the chili, _____ it was far too salty.

> REMEMBER YOUR COORDINATING CONJUNCTIONS WITH **FANBOYS** OR THE MNEMONIC PHRASE: "**S**CARY **O**WLS **A**RE **N**EVER **F**AR **B**EHIND **Y**OU."

WHAT IS A PREPOSITION?

A **PREPOSITION** SHOWS THE RELATIONSHIP BETWEEN A NOUN OR PRONOUN AND SOME OTHER WORD IN A SENTENCE.

The giraffe twisted her neck **around** the tree to get the best leaf.

AROUND EXPLAINS WHERE THE GIRAFFE'S NECK IS IN RELATION TO THE TREE.

The giraffe stood **over** the watering hole.

HMMM...

Who knows what dangers lurk **beneath** the water's surface?

SPOTTED STEAK FOR DINNER TONIGHT?

Brain Challenge: Using the examples above, brainstorm a list of words that you think could be **prepositions**. Check your answers on page 25.

_____

_____

_____

Possible answers: For example, if **over** is a preposition, maybe **under** is too!

24

www.super-ela.com/terms/prepositions

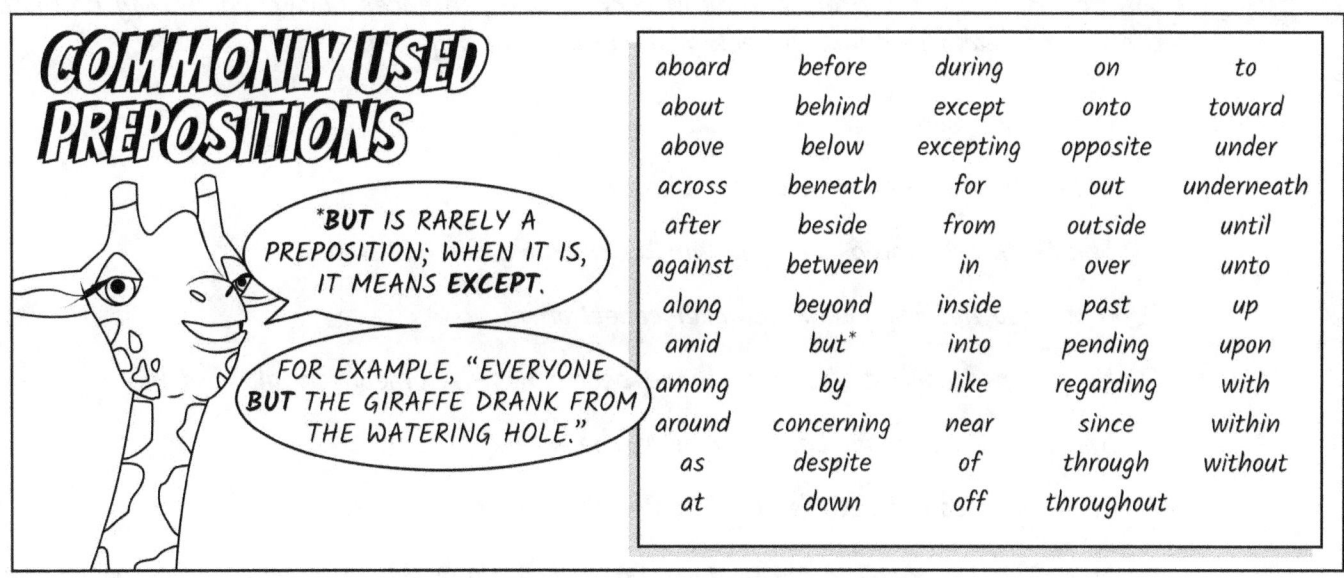

COMMONLY USED PREPOSITIONS

*BUT IS RARELY A PREPOSITION; WHEN IT IS, IT MEANS EXCEPT.

FOR EXAMPLE, "EVERYONE BUT THE GIRAFFE DRANK FROM THE WATERING HOLE."

aboard	before	during	on	to
about	behind	except	onto	toward
above	below	excepting	opposite	under
across	beneath	for	out	underneath
after	beside	from	outside	until
against	between	in	over	unto
along	beyond	inside	past	up
amid	but*	into	pending	upon
among	by	like	regarding	with
around	concerning	near	since	within
as	despite	of	through	without
at	down	off	throughout	

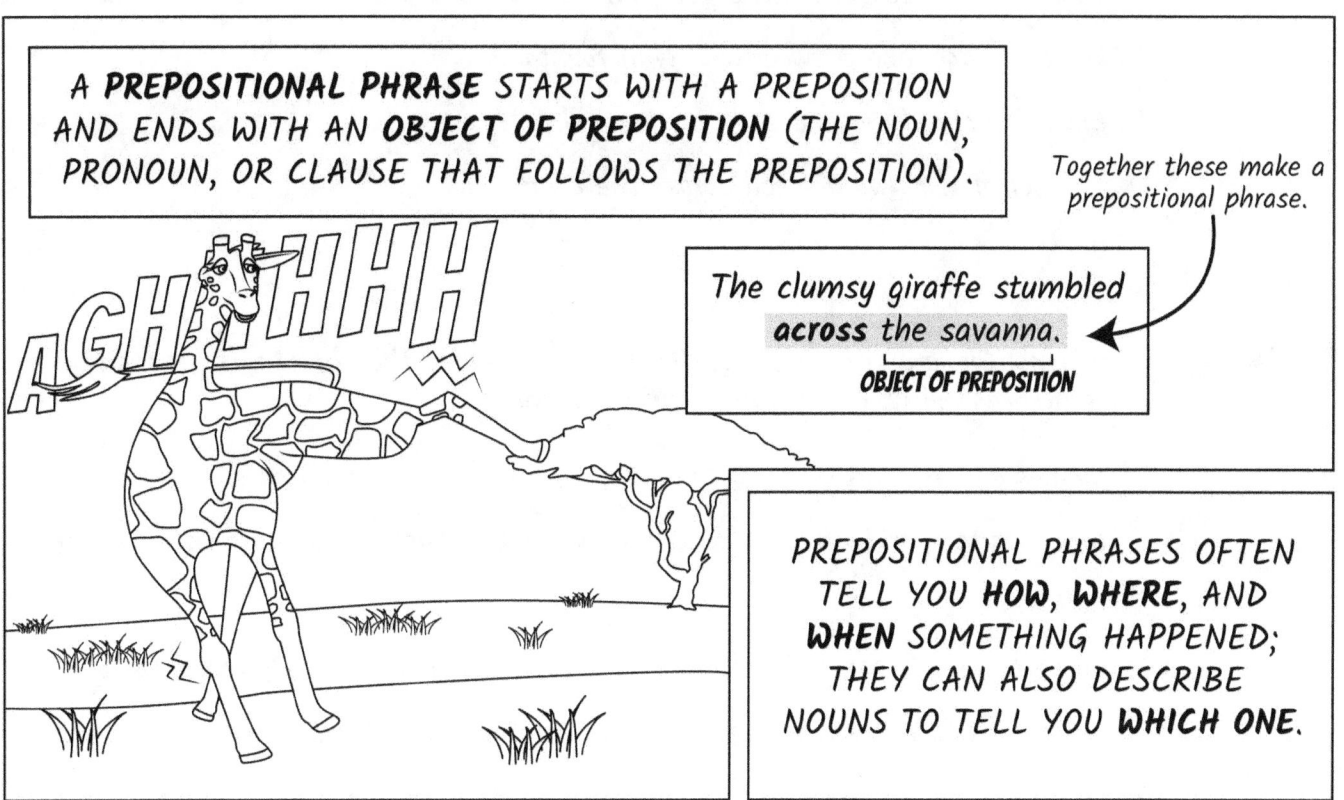

A **PREPOSITIONAL PHRASE** STARTS WITH A PREPOSITION AND ENDS WITH AN **OBJECT OF PREPOSITION** (THE NOUN, PRONOUN, OR CLAUSE THAT FOLLOWS THE PREPOSITION).

Together these make a prepositional phrase.

The clumsy giraffe stumbled **across** the savanna.
OBJECT OF PREPOSITION

PREPOSITIONAL PHRASES OFTEN TELL YOU **HOW**, **WHERE**, AND **WHEN** SOMETHING HAPPENED; THEY CAN ALSO DESCRIBE NOUNS TO TELL YOU **WHICH ONE**.

Brain Challenge: Choose two **prepositions** from the list above. Write two sentences that use prepositions. Circle each preposition you use.

_____

_____

_____

Possible answers: 1) Elgin lives **among** the giraffes. 2) D'arcy is short enough to walk **under** a giraffe.

www.super-ela.com/terms/prepositions

EXERCISE 15 **Directions:** Circle the **prepositions** in each of the sentences below. There may be more than one in each sentence! Check your answers on page 34.

1. Dinner was served at six o'clock.
2. Gina couldn't sleep without her blanket.
3. The team celebrated their big win by splurging for milkshakes.
4. I love you despite your nutcracker collection.
5. He slumped against the tree on the beach, hoping someone would find him.
6. Should we eat dinner before or after the movie?
7. The cats meowed outside the kitchen all evening.
8. Sebastian explored the entire park; he walked along the river's edge, underneath the kissing bridge, and between the twin fountains.
9. Eleanor dropped her phone down the well.
10. The ball flew at warp speed across the court.

EXERCISE 16 **Directions:** Circle all of the **prepositions** and underline the **objects of preposition** in the sentences below. Check your answers on page 34.

1. Llamas are from South America, and they graze in the mountains.
2. Great white sharks are plentiful in the waters of Australia and off the coast of California.
3. Marie Curie, née Maria Sklodowska, was born in Poland in 1867; she is famous for her contributions to science in the areas of physics and radioactivity.
4. Daniel couldn't pry the bread from the roof of his mouth; it was plastered there with copious amounts of peanut butter.
5. Abby wanted to go ice fishing, but she couldn't tell a fishing pole from a net, and she was afraid she would get stuck inside the ice shack.

WHAT IS AN INTERJECTION?

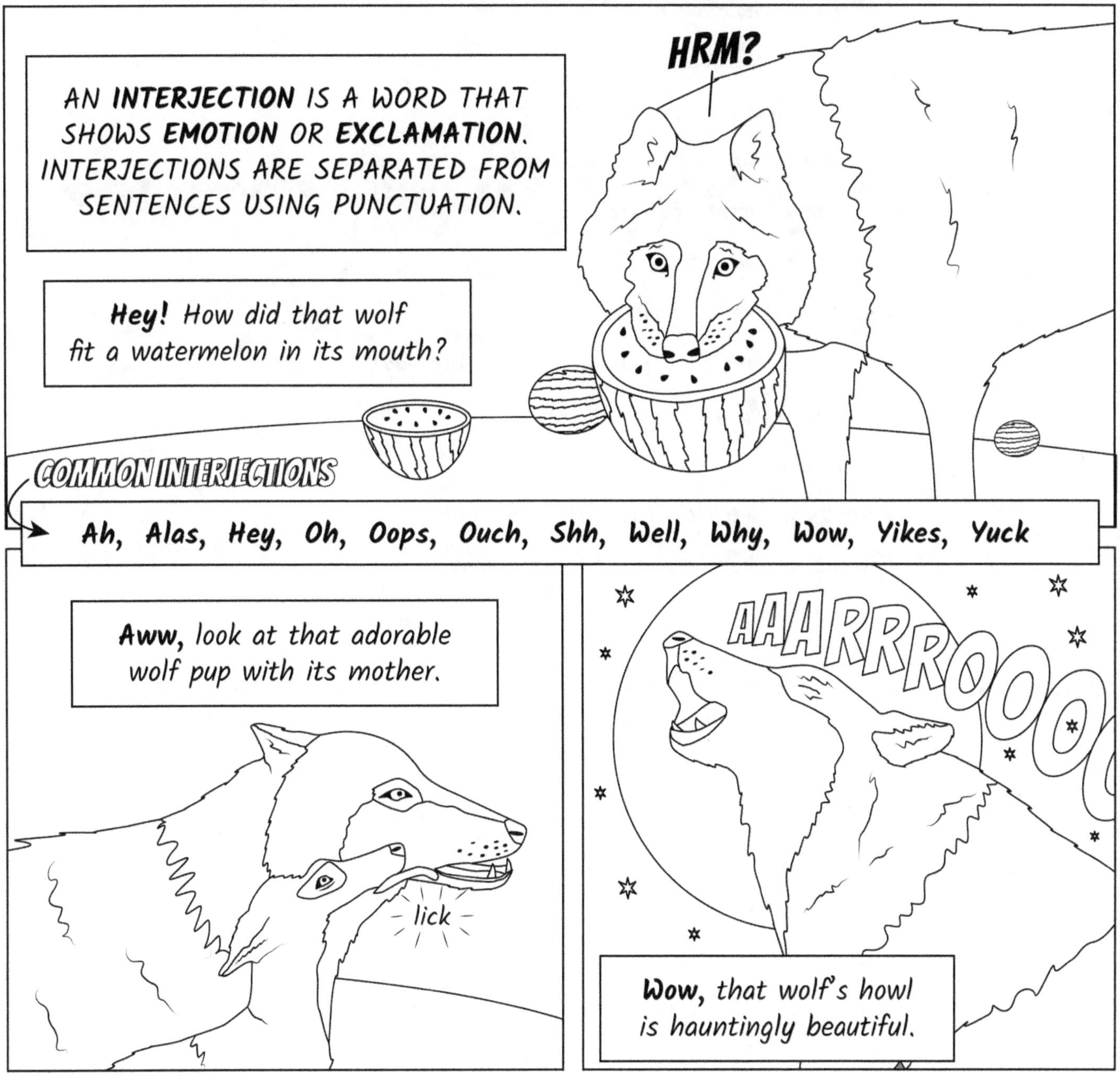

An **INTERJECTION** is a word that shows **EMOTION** or **EXCLAMATION**. Interjections are separated from sentences using punctuation.

HRM?

Hey! How did that wolf fit a watermelon in its mouth?

COMMON INTERJECTIONS
Ah, Alas, Hey, Oh, Oops, Ouch, Shh, Well, Why, Wow, Yikes, Yuck

Aww, look at that adorable wolf pup with its mother.

-lick-

AAARRROOOO

Wow, that wolf's howl is hauntingly beautiful.

Brain Challenge: Read and color the comic above. Then cover it with a piece of paper. Next, think about how you would explain **interjections** to a friend. Write your answer on the lines below. No peeking! Check your knowledge when you're finished.

_____
_____
_____

www.super-ela.com/terms/interjections

EXERCISE 17 **Directions:** Circle the **interjections** in the sentences below. Check your answers on page 35.

1. Oh, that's what you meant.
2. Well! I suppose you want half of my sandwich.
3. This assignment is too difficult. Ugh!
4. Wow, you really do have a pet tiger.
5. Hey, can I borrow your stapler?
6. Whew, it's freezing out there!
7. Whee! I love roller coasters!
8. Phooey! I didn't want a ham sandwich anyway.
9. Ouch! Why did you pinch me?
10. This is a library. Shh!
11. Alas, she was too tired to brush her teeth.
12. Psst, do you have a pencil I could borrow?

EXERCISE 18 **Directions:** Replace each blank below with an appropriate **interjection** from the following list. Remember to add punctuation. Check your answers on page 35.

| Mmm | Ah | Alas | Egads |
| Psst | Whew | Shh | Ouch |

1. _____ that was an incredible croissant.
2. _____ it is the last day of the season for our ping pong league.
3. _____ The dishwasher is overflowing with soap suds!
4. _____ That was a close call.
5. _____ the baby is sleeping.
6. _____ can you pass this note to Stacy?
7. _____ that's where I left my pop tart.
8. _____ I stubbed my toe!

WHAT DID YOU LEARN?

Revisit the inventory you made on page 1 where you described **1) what you already knew about the parts of speech** and **2) what you wanted to learn**. Now that you've completed the exercises in this workbook, reflect on your learning. On the lines below, write down what you've added to your knowledge about the parts of speech. Did the exercises help you learn what you wanted to know? What else do you want to know now that you're an expert in the parts of speech?

_____
_____
_____
_____
_____
_____
_____
_____
_____
_____
_____
_____
_____
_____
_____

ANSWER KEY

EXERCISE 1 ANSWERS (NOUNS)

There was once a **rhinoceros** named **Dave**. He was a sweet **pachyderm**, unlike his **brothers**, **Luke** and **William**. While his **siblings** roamed the **savanna** looking for **trouble** in the **form** of taunting **zebras** and harassing **lions**, **Dave** spent his **time** planting a lovely **garden** and chatting with his **neighbors**, the **wildebeest** and the **ostrich**. He was especially nice to the **warthog**, as he admired her beautiful **tusks** and stately **gait**. To show her his **admiration**, **Dave** brought the **warthog bouquets** of **flowers** and sweet **grasses**. Because of these **actions**, **Dave** earned the **reputation** of being the nicest **beast** in the **region**.

EXERCISE 2 ANSWERS (COMMON NOUNS)

Answers will vary but should describe common items or animals in the suggested category.

1. (birds) flamingo, ostrich, owl, hummingbird, **seagull**, **albatross**, **emu**
2. (vegetables) carrot, lettuce, potato, pepper, **squash**, **radish**, **cucumber**
3. (farm animals) cow, pig, horse, sheep, **donkey**, **duck**, **chicken**
4. (cheeses) cheddar, provolone, mozzarella, parmesan, **gouda**, **gorgonzola**, **feta**
5. (ocean creatures) fish, narwhal, whale, seahorse, **octopus**, **shark**, **stingray**

EXERCISE 3 ANSWERS (PROPER AND COMMON NOUNS)

1. Green Bay Packers (d. team)
2. Australia (b. country)
3. Ludwig van Beethoven (a. composer)
4. Mississippi River (e. river)
5. Loch Ness Monster (c. mythical creature)

EXERCISE 4 ANSWERS (PERSONAL PRONOUNS - SUBJECT AND OBJECT)

1. **She** loves karate.
2. **They** prefer goat cheese pizza.
3. Gloria and John walked with **them**.
4. **I** hope that tiger isn't following **us**.
5. Eloise taunted **him**, but **we** put a stop to it.
6. Can you ask **her** if **she** will go to the movies with **me**?
7. **He** is less agile than **she**.
8. Have you seen my bicycle? I can't find **it**!

EXERCISE 5 ANSWERS (PERSONAL AND POSSESSIVE PRONOUNS)

1. ~~Us~~ **We** must return this lost jacket to ~~it's~~ **its** owner.
2. This cardigan is mine! (✓)
3. ~~There~~ **Their** potato salad is the best ~~me~~ **I** have ever tasted!
4. ~~He's~~ **His** basketball jersey is in the washing machine.
5. ~~You're~~ **Your** mom told ~~me~~ **my** mom to tell ~~I~~ **me** to tell ~~your~~ **you** that ~~her~~ **she** is making a casserole for dinner.

EXERCISE 6 ANSWERS (VERBS AND VERB TENSES)

1. Denise **bakes** bread every morning at five o'clock. **(present tense)**
2. She **perfected** her recipe over many years of practice. **(past tense)**
3. Denise **sells** her bread in a little shop on the edge of town. **(present tense)**
4. In the morning, her store **will bustle** with customers. **(future tense)**
5. The townspeople **love** her bread; it **tastes** of cinnamon! **(present tense)**
6. Only one person—a stranger—**expressed** dislike for the cinnamon bread. **(past tense)**
7. He **had** a cinnamon allergy. **(past tense)**
8. Denise **will think** about how to help this stranger. **(future tense)**
9. She **created** a cinnamon-free loaf. **(past tense)**
10. The stranger **thanked** her, **paid** for the bread, and **scarfed** it down. **(past tense)**

EXERCISE 7 ANSWERS (TO BE LINKING VERBS)

1. On average, Florida **is** one of the hottest states in the U.S.
2. Zora Neale Hurston, a noted writer of the Harlem Renaissance era, **was** an award-winning author who wrote classics like <u>Their Eyes Were Watching God</u>.
3. Killer whales, also called orcas, **have been** misunderstood for many years, likely owing to their menacing name.
4. This is hard to admit, but I **am** afraid of Jell-O and other gelatinous desserts.
5. Bees **are** important for the world's ecosystem, as they help pollinate crops.
6. Despite the fact that it **was** enormous—weighing in at over 30,000lbs—the Tyrannosaurus rex's arms were only three feet long.
7. Socrates, Plato, and Aristotle **were** Greek philosophers who lived more than 2,400 years ago.

EXERCISE 8 ANSWERS (LINKING VS. ACTION VERBS)

1. Much to her surprise, Regina **thought** the seaweed and clam chowder **tasted** delicious.
                                          ACTION   LINKING
2. Torrey **feels** bored after three hours of notetaking in Mr. Bertram's history class.
           LINKING
3. An enormous talking robot **appeared** to Regan in a dream; he **claimed** his name **was** "Optimus Prime,"
                                          ACTION   ACTION   LINKING

   but his nametag **read** "Larry."
                      ACTION
4. To Elijah the field of daisies **seemed** endless; in reality, it **was** a small garden in his backyard.
                                 LINKING   LINKING
5. Heather **tasted** a small bite of the raw fish before deciding that it **was** safe to eat.
              ACTION   LINKING
6. Seconds from sleep, Eloise **felt** her mother **place** the soft blanket over her.
                             ACTION   ACTION
7. With contents like moldy socks and putrefied cabbage, it **was** no wonder that the garbage in the
                                                                            LINKING

   alleyway **smelled** rotten.
               LINKING

EXERCISE 9 ANSWERS (ADJECTIVES)

1. A **sweet** smell wafted through the air.
2. Was it **chocolate** cookies or **fresh** brownies?
3. Caroline couldn't tell, but she knew she wanted whatever **delicious** treat was in the kitchen.
4. She crept, **silent** as a mouse, toward the **open kitchen** door.
5. **Her** mom stooped in front of **their enormous** oven, pulling out a **mystery** pan from **its warm** interior.
6. Mom didn't know **little** Caroline was hiding by the door.
7. When she turned around and saw **creepy** eyes peering from the **black** hallway, she was startled.
8. She dropped the **entire** tray of cookies on the **kitchen** floor.
9. "Oh no!" Caroline cried as she emerged to help **her** mother pick up the **broken** cookies.
10. "Thank you, Caroline," **her** mom said with a **disappointed** note in **her** voice.

EXERCISE 10 ANSWERS (POSITIVE, COMPARATIVE, AND SUPERLATIVE ADJECTIVES)

1. Yesterday's lunch was **tasty**.
2. It was the **tastiest** of all the lunches I've ever eaten!
3. Is your lunch **tastier** than mine?
4. Four is **greater** than five.

5. Of all the numbers between one and infinity, which is the **greatest**?
6. Thirteen is not a **great** number when it comes to luck!
7. Hercules was the **strongest** of the Greek heroes.
8. He was **stronger** than Achilles because he didn't have a weak ankle.
9. Though he was **strong**, he wasn't very bright.
10. Gerald wanted to be **better** at math than his brother, Hank.
11. Unfortunately for Gerald, Hank was the **best** mathlete in the nation, so he was going to be hard to beat.
12. Gerald settled for just being **good** at math.
13. Natalie was an **inventive** child.
14. She wanted to push her abilities so that she would be **more inventive** than her hero, Nikola Tesla.
15. "Someday," she thought, "I'll be the **most inventive** scientist the world has ever seen!

EXERCISE 11 ANSWERS (ADVERBS)

1. The bear (smiled) **politely** at the camper, hoping it would ease her fear.
   VERB
2. You are **almost** (always) welcome to eat at our house; the only exception is when we have company.
   ADVERB
3. The platypus is an **extremely** (curious) creature with its avian nose and mammalian body.
   ADJECTIVE
4. In addition to synchronized swimming, Janine **also** (enjoys) spelunking, or cave diving.
   VERB
5. Ariel is **often** (considered) the most talented ballerina in her class.
   ADJECTIVE

EXERCISE 12 ANSWERS (ADVERBS)

1. Marcus has some **very** interesting questions about last night's homework.
2. I **sometimes** wonder if there is a perfect flavor of ice cream.
3. The alligator swam **slowly** across the pond.
4. It is **generally** wise to save money for a rainy day.
5. The pizza was **extremely** hot, and the cheese burned the roof of Andrew's mouth.
6. I **almost** never eat breakfast in bed.

EXERCISE 13 ANSWERS (COORDINATING CONJUNCTIONS)

1. Sookie wore a beautiful hat trimmed with white **and** green feathers.
2. The cat wanted to eat the mouse, **yet** she was too lazy to get up.
3. Dante was fluent in Spanish **but** not in French.
4. Regina couldn't decide if she wanted three cookies **or** four cookies, **so** she just ate seven cookies.

5. The elephant cried all morning, **for** it had a chipped tusk.
6. Bernard couldn't sing, **nor** could he dance.

EXERCISE 14 ANSWERS (COORDINATING CONJUNCTIONS)

1. Chloe wasn't cold, **nor** was she hot.
2. Lightning split the old oak tree in two, **so** it had to be removed.
3. I want to do my homework, **but** I can't because I'm watching television!
4. Flamingos are usually a combination of white **and** pink; they become pinker if they eat more shrimp!
5. The dogs looked pleadingly at their owner, **for** it was time for dinner.
6. Daniel couldn't decide if he wanted to dye his hair navy **or** aqua.
7. The ground was frozen **and** hard, **so** it was not a good time to install a fence.
8. Tracy tried to eat the chili, **but** it was far too salty.

EXERCISE 15 ANSWERS (PREPOSITIONS)

1. Dinner was served **at** six o'clock.
2. Gina couldn't sleep **without** her blanket.
3. The team celebrated their big win **by** splurging **for** milkshakes.
4. I love you **despite** your nutcracker collection.
5. He slumped **against** the tree **on** the beach, hoping someone would find him.
6. Should we eat dinner **before** or **after** the movie?
7. The cats meowed **outside** the kitchen all evening.
8. Sebastian explored the entire park; he walked **along** the river's edge, **underneath** the kissing bridge, and **between** the twin fountains.
9. Eleanor dropped her phone **down** the well.
10. The ball flew **at** warp speed **across** the court.

EXERCISE 16 ANSWERS (PREPOSITIONS AND PREPOSITIONAL PHRASES)

1. Llamas are **from** South America, and they graze **in** the mountains.
2. Great white sharks are plentiful **in** the waters **of** Australia and **off** the coast **of** California.
3. Marie Curie, née Maria Sklodowska, was born **in** Poland **in** 1867; she is famous **for** her contributions **to** science **in** the areas **of** physics and radioactivity.
4. Daniel couldn't pry the bread **from** the roof **of** his mouth; it was plastered there **with** copious amounts **of** peanut butter.

5. Abby wanted to go ice fishing, but she couldn't tell a fishing pole **from** <u>a net</u>, and she was afraid she would get stuck **inside** <u>the ice shack</u>.

EXERCISE 17 ANSWERS (INTERJECTIONS)

1. **Oh,** that's what you meant.
2. **Well!** I suppose you want half of my sandwich.
3. This assignment is too difficult. **Ugh!**
4. **Wow,** you really do have a pet tiger.
5. **Hey,** can I borrow your stapler?
6. **Whew,** it's freezing out there!
7. **Whee!** I love roller coasters!
8. **Phooey!** I didn't want a ham sandwich anyway.
9. **Ouch!** Why did you pinch me?
10. This is a library. **Shh!**
11. **Alas,** she was too tired to brush her teeth.
12. **Psst,** do you have a pencil I could borrow?

EXERCISE 18 ANSWERS (INTERJECTIONS)

1. **Mmm,** that was an incredible croissant.
2. **Alas,** it is the last day of the season for our ping pong league.
3. **Egads!** The dishwasher is overflowing with soap suds!
4. **Whew!** That was a close call.
5. **Shh,** the baby is sleeping.
6. **Psst,** can you pass this note to Stacy?
7. **Ah,** that's where I left my pop tart.
8. **Ouch!** I stubbed my toe!

TURN THE PAGE FOR SUPER SECRET BONUS CONTENT...

WHAT IS A MAIN CLAUSE?

A **MAIN**, OR **INDEPENDENT**, CLAUSE CAN STAND ON ITS OWN AS A COMPLETE SENTENCE. A MAIN CLAUSE MUST CONTAIN A **SUBJECT** AND A **VERB**.

A **VERB** EXPRESSES AN ACTION.

THE **SUBJECT** IS THE WHO OR WHAT THAT DOES THE ACTION.

MAIN CLAUSE
Aliens breakdance in the moonlight.

ALIENS = **THE SUBJECT**
BREAKDANCE = **THE VERB**

MAIN CLAUSE
They love music with a beat.

THEY = **THE SUBJECT**
LOVE = **THE VERB**

IF A SENTENCE DOES NOT HAVE A MAIN CLAUSE, IT IS A **FRAGMENT**.

Brain Challenge: Write two main clauses. Use the **verb** "sing" in your first main clause, and use the **subject** "Lucinda" in your second main clause.

_____

_____

_____

Possible answers: 1) Birds sing sweet songs in the morning. 2) Lucinda claims she was abducted by aliens.

MAIN CLAUSE PRACTICE

Directions: In each of the following sentences, circle the **subject** and underline the **verb**. Cover the answers below with a sheet of paper until you're ready to check your work.

1. Your kitchen is overrun with puppies.
2. He hid the peanut butter.
3. Mrs. Fletcher wants more juice.
4. Alex trampled the begonias.
5. The cat sulked in the corner.
6. Marcy broke my camera!
7. Danny loves dinosaurs.
8. We have enough food for everyone.
9. Olivia explained how to wrap a present.
10. Lifeguards closed the beach because of red tide.

MAIN CLAUSE PRACTICE ANSWERS

1. (Your kitchen) is overrun with puppies.
2. (He) hid the peanut butter.
3. (Mrs. Fletcher) wants more juice.
4. (Alex) trampled the begonias.
5. (The cat) sulked in the corner.
6. (Marcy) broke my camera!
7. (Danny) loves dinosaurs.
8. (We) have enough food for everyone.
9. (Olivia) explained how to wrap a present.
10. (Lifeguards) closed the beach because of red tide.

WHAT IS A SUBORDINATE CLAUSE?

A **SUBORDINATE**, OR **DEPENDENT**, CLAUSE HAS A SUBJECT AND A VERB, BUT IT **CANNOT** STAND ALONE AS A SENTENCE. A SUBORDINATE CLAUSE MUST BE USED WITH A **MAIN CLAUSE** IN ORDER TO MAKE SENSE.

A SUBORDINATE CLAUSE DOESN'T PROVIDE A COMPLETE THOUGHT. IT LEAVES THE READER WONDERING, "SO, WHAT HAPPENS NEXT?"

FOR EXAMPLE

If I beat that cow in a staring contest.

SUBJECT   VERB

WHAT WILL HAPPEN **IF** YOU WIN?

ATTACH A MAIN CLAUSE TO A SUBORDINATE CLAUSE TO COMPLETE THE THOUGHT.

OPEN YOUR EYES, LOOK UP TO THE SKIES AND SEEEEEEEE!

FIXED VERSION

If I beat that cow in a staring contest, **it will sing Queen's "Bohemian Rhapsody."**

HOW TO SPOT A SUBORDINATE CLAUSE

Subordinate clauses typically begin with **subordinating conjunctions, relative pronouns,** or **relative adverbs**.

SUBORDINATING CONJUNCTION EXAMPLES

after	although	as	because
before	even though	if	provided that
since	though	unless	until
when	while	whenever	whereas

38

www.super-ela.com terms/subordinate-clauses/

SUBORDINATING CONJUNCTION EXAMPLE

Aliens abduct cows **because they admire their spots.**

AGAIN?

MAIN CLAUSE — Aliens abduct cows — SUBJECT VERB

SUBORDINATE CLAUSE — because they admire their spots — SUBORDINATING CONJUNCTION, SUBJECT, VERB

Brain Challenge: Complete the following sentence by adding a **subordinating conjunction**. Next, label the **main** and **subordinate clauses**.

_____ the aliens abducted my favorite cow, I decided to raise pigs instead.

Answer: After; Main Clause = I decided to raise pigs instead, Subordinate Clause = After the aliens abducted my favorite cow

www.super-ela.com terms/subordinate-clauses/

RELATIVE PRONOUN EXAMPLES

| that | who | whose | which |
| whoever | whom | whomever | whichever |

RELATIVE PRONOUN EXAMPLE

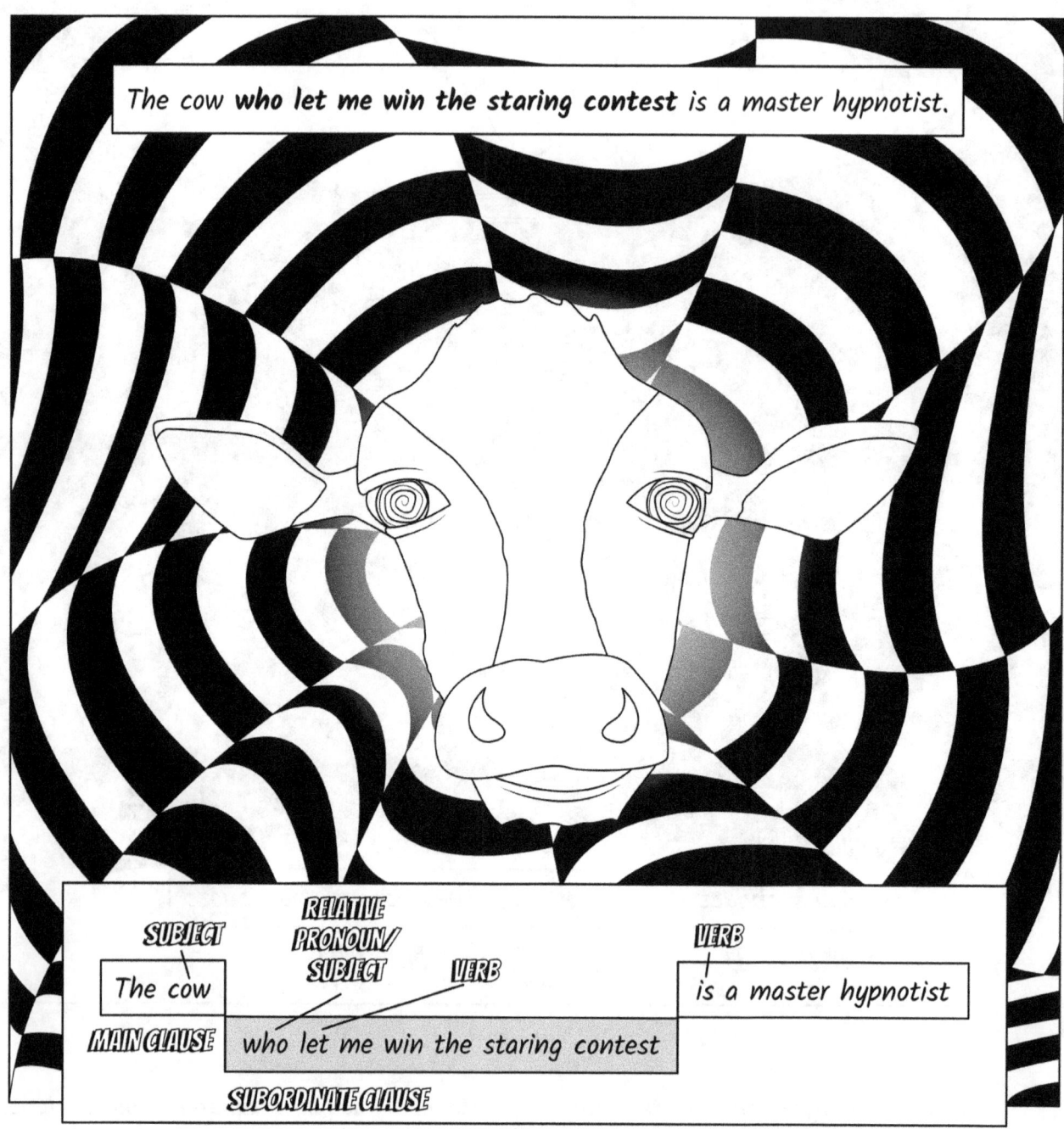

Brain Challenge: Complete the following sentence by adding a **relative pronoun**. Next, label the **main** and **subordinate clauses**.

I applaud _____ trained this cow in hypnotism.

Answer: whoever. Main Clause = I applaud, Subordinate Clause = whoever trained this cow in hypnotism

RELATIVE ADVERB EXAMPLES
when   where   why

RELATIVE ADVERB EXAMPLE

Brain Challenge: Complete the following sentence by adding a **relative adverb**. Next, label the **main** and **subordinate clauses**.

I don't know _____ the aliens keep abducting my cows.

Answer: why; Main Clause = I don't know, Subordinate Clause = why the aliens keep abducting my cows

SUBORDINATE CLAUSE PRACTICE

Directions: In each of the following sentences, underline the **subordinate clause**. Then, identify if the clause starts with a **subordinating conjunction**, **relative pronoun**, or **relative adverb**. Cover the answers below with a sheet of paper until you're ready to check your work.

1. I know a wolverine who performs magic tricks.
2. Ghosts cannot tan because they are translucent.
3. When they are hungry, sheep prefer pizza.
4. The sheep who steals my pizza is hanging around the yard again.
5. Though werewolves are cute, they make poor pets.
6. Even though they always look fabulous, unicorns never pose for pictures.
7. After the tiger snarled, the movie theater became silent.
8. Will you fix the trampoline while I sunbathe by the pool?
9. We can de-gnome the garden today unless you have other plans.
10. I want to know where you bought that garden gnome!

SUBORDINATE CLAUSE PRACTICE ANSWERS

1. I know a wolverine <u>who performs magic tricks</u>.
   RELATIVE PRONOUN
2. Ghosts cannot tan <u>because they are translucent</u>.
   SUBORDINATING CONJUNCTION
3. <u>When they are hungry</u>, sheep prefer pizza.
   RELATIVE ADVERB
4. The sheep <u>who steals my pizza</u> is hanging around the yard again.
   RELATIVE PRONOUN
5. <u>Though werewolves are cute</u>, they make poor pets.
   SUBORDINATING CONJUNCTION
6. <u>Even though they always look fabulous</u>, unicorns never pose for pictures.
   SUBORDINATING CONJUNCTION
7. <u>After the tiger snarled</u>, the movie theater became silent.
   SUBORDINATING CONJUNCTION
8. Will you fix the trampoline <u>while I sunbathe by the pool</u>?
   SUBORDINATING CONJUNCTION
9. We can de-gnome the garden today <u>unless you have other plans</u>.
   SUBORDINATING CONJUNCTION
10. I want to know <u>where you bought that garden gnome</u>!
    RELATIVE ADVERB